# Blog Growth PLANNER

Finances & key analytics annual tracker

*Ana Skyes*

COPYRIGHT © 2021 ANA SKYES
THE SHE APPROACH
ALL RIGHTS RESERVED.

# DEDICATION

This planner is dedicated to all bloggers and content creators looking to get intentional about their blog growth. It all starts with you keeping track of your monthly finances and blog analytics. And this planner is designed to help you do just that.

Write down your goals, plan your entire year at a glance and optimize the time you spend blogging to get maximum impact, grow your online brand and increase your revenue. Because the numbers don't lie!

# CONTENTS

| | |
|---|---|
| Calendars | 7 |
| Sample pages | 9 |
| Goal setting pages | 13 |
|     Your year at a glance | 14 |
|     Annual income goals | 16 |
|     Milestone income tracker | 17 |
|     Blog growth goals | 18 |
| Useful trackers | 20 |
|     Blog post content trakcer | 21 |
|     Accounts & login info | 23 |
|     Affiliate programs tracker | 25 |
| Mapping out your prices & offers | 26 |
| Annual trackers | 35 |
|     Income tracker | 36 |
|     Blog traffic tracker | 37 |
|     Social reach tracker | 38 |
| Monthly planners | 39 |
| Annual review | 196 |
| About the author | 202 |

# 2022

## JANUARY
| MO | TU | WE | TH | FR | SA | SU |
|----|----|----|----|----|----|----|
|    |    |    |    |    | 1  | 2  |
| 3  | 4  | 5  | 6  | 7  | 8  | 9  |
| 10 | 11 | 12 | 13 | 14 | 15 | 16 |
| 17 | 18 | 19 | 20 | 21 | 22 | 23 |
| 24 | 25 | 26 | 27 | 28 | 29 | 30 |
| 31 |    |    |    |    |    |    |

## FEBRUARY
| MO | TU | WE | TH | FR | SA | SU |
|----|----|----|----|----|----|----|
|    | 1  | 2  | 3  | 4  | 5  | 6  |
| 7  | 8  | 9  | 10 | 11 | 12 | 13 |
| 14 | 15 | 16 | 17 | 18 | 19 | 20 |
| 21 | 22 | 23 | 24 | 25 | 26 | 27 |
| 28 |    |    |    |    |    |    |

## MARCH
| MO | TU | WE | TH | FR | SA | SU |
|----|----|----|----|----|----|----|
|    | 1  | 2  | 3  | 4  | 5  | 6  |
| 7  | 8  | 9  | 10 | 11 | 12 | 13 |
| 14 | 15 | 16 | 17 | 18 | 19 | 20 |
| 21 | 22 | 23 | 24 | 25 | 26 | 27 |
| 28 | 29 | 30 | 31 |    |    |    |

## APRIL
| MO | TU | WE | TH | FR | SA | SU |
|----|----|----|----|----|----|----|
|    |    |    |    | 1  | 2  | 3  |
| 4  | 5  | 6  | 7  | 8  | 9  | 10 |
| 11 | 12 | 13 | 14 | 15 | 16 | 17 |
| 18 | 19 | 20 | 21 | 22 | 23 | 24 |
| 25 | 26 | 27 | 28 | 29 | 30 |    |

## MAY
| MO | TU | WE | TH | FR | SA | SU |
|----|----|----|----|----|----|----|
|    |    |    |    |    |    | 1  |
| 2  | 3  | 4  | 5  | 6  | 7  | 8  |
| 9  | 10 | 11 | 12 | 13 | 14 | 15 |
| 16 | 17 | 18 | 19 | 20 | 21 | 22 |
| 23 | 24 | 25 | 26 | 27 | 28 | 29 |
| 30 | 31 |    |    |    |    |    |

## JUNE
| MO | TU | WE | TH | FR | SA | SU |
|----|----|----|----|----|----|----|
|    |    | 1  | 2  | 3  | 4  | 5  |
| 6  | 7  | 8  | 9  | 10 | 11 | 12 |
| 13 | 14 | 15 | 16 | 17 | 18 | 19 |
| 20 | 21 | 22 | 23 | 24 | 25 | 26 |
| 27 | 28 | 29 | 30 |    |    |    |

## JULY
| MO | TU | WE | TH | FR | SA | SU |
|----|----|----|----|----|----|----|
|    |    |    |    | 1  | 2  | 3  |
| 4  | 5  | 6  | 7  | 8  | 9  | 10 |
| 11 | 12 | 13 | 14 | 15 | 16 | 17 |
| 18 | 19 | 20 | 21 | 22 | 23 | 24 |
| 25 | 26 | 27 | 28 | 29 | 30 | 31 |

## AUGUST
| MO | TU | WE | TH | FR | SA | SU |
|----|----|----|----|----|----|----|
| 1  | 2  | 3  | 4  | 5  | 6  | 7  |
| 8  | 9  | 10 | 11 | 12 | 13 | 14 |
| 15 | 16 | 17 | 18 | 19 | 20 | 21 |
| 22 | 23 | 24 | 25 | 26 | 27 | 28 |
| 29 | 30 | 31 |    |    |    |    |

## SEPTEMBER
| MO | TU | WE | TH | FR | SA | SU |
|----|----|----|----|----|----|----|
|    |    |    | 1  | 2  | 3  | 4  |
| 5  | 6  | 7  | 8  | 9  | 10 | 11 |
| 12 | 13 | 14 | 15 | 16 | 17 | 18 |
| 19 | 20 | 21 | 22 | 23 | 24 | 25 |
| 26 | 27 | 28 | 29 | 30 |    |    |

## OCTOBER
| MO | TU | WE | TH | FR | SA | SU |
|----|----|----|----|----|----|----|
|    |    |    |    |    | 1  | 2  |
| 3  | 4  | 5  | 6  | 7  | 8  | 9  |
| 10 | 11 | 12 | 13 | 14 | 15 | 16 |
| 17 | 18 | 19 | 20 | 21 | 22 | 23 |
| 24 | 25 | 26 | 27 | 28 | 29 | 30 |
| 31 |    |    |    |    |    |    |

## NOVEMBER
| MO | TU | WE | TH | FR | SA | SU |
|----|----|----|----|----|----|----|
|    | 1  | 2  | 3  | 4  | 5  | 6  |
| 7  | 8  | 9  | 10 | 11 | 12 | 13 |
| 14 | 15 | 16 | 17 | 18 | 19 | 20 |
| 21 | 22 | 23 | 24 | 25 | 26 | 27 |
| 28 | 29 | 30 |    |    |    |    |

## DECEMBER
| MO | TU | WE | TH | FR | SA | SU |
|----|----|----|----|----|----|----|
|    |    |    | 1  | 2  | 3  | 4  |
| 5  | 6  | 7  | 8  | 9  | 10 | 11 |
| 12 | 13 | 14 | 15 | 16 | 17 | 18 |
| 19 | 20 | 21 | 22 | 23 | 24 | 25 |
| 26 | 27 | 28 | 29 | 30 | 31 |    |

# 2023

### JANUARY

| MO | TU | WE | TH | FR | SA | SU |
|----|----|----|----|----|----|----|
|    |    |    |    |    |    | 1  |
| 2  | 3  | 4  | 5  | 6  | 7  | 8  |
| 9  | 10 | 11 | 12 | 13 | 14 | 15 |
| 16 | 17 | 18 | 19 | 20 | 21 | 22 |
| 23 | 24 | 25 | 26 | 27 | 28 | 29 |
| 30 | 31 |    |    |    |    |    |

### FEBRUARY

| MO | TU | WE | TH | FR | SA | SU |
|----|----|----|----|----|----|----|
|    |    | 1  | 2  | 3  | 4  | 5  |
| 6  | 7  | 8  | 9  | 10 | 11 | 12 |
| 13 | 14 | 15 | 16 | 17 | 18 | 19 |
| 20 | 21 | 22 | 23 | 24 | 25 | 26 |
| 27 | 28 |    |    |    |    |    |

### MARCH

| MO | TU | WE | TH | FR | SA | SU |
|----|----|----|----|----|----|----|
|    |    | 1  | 2  | 3  | 4  | 5  |
| 6  | 7  | 8  | 9  | 10 | 11 | 12 |
| 13 | 14 | 15 | 16 | 17 | 18 | 19 |
| 20 | 21 | 22 | 23 | 24 | 25 | 26 |
| 27 | 28 | 29 | 30 | 31 |    |    |

### APRIL

| MO | TU | WE | TH | FR | SA | SU |
|----|----|----|----|----|----|----|
|    |    |    |    |    | 1  | 2  |
| 3  | 4  | 5  | 6  | 7  | 8  | 9  |
| 10 | 11 | 12 | 13 | 14 | 15 | 16 |
| 17 | 18 | 19 | 20 | 21 | 22 | 23 |
| 24 | 25 | 26 | 27 | 28 | 29 | 30 |

### MAY

| MO | TU | WE | TH | FR | SA | SU |
|----|----|----|----|----|----|----|
| 1  | 2  | 3  | 4  | 5  | 6  | 7  |
| 8  | 9  | 10 | 11 | 12 | 13 | 14 |
| 15 | 16 | 17 | 18 | 19 | 20 | 21 |
| 22 | 23 | 24 | 25 | 26 | 27 | 28 |
| 29 | 30 | 31 |    |    |    |    |

### JUNE

| MO | TU | WE | TH | FR | SA | SU |
|----|----|----|----|----|----|----|
|    |    |    | 1  | 2  | 3  | 4  |
| 5  | 6  | 7  | 8  | 9  | 10 | 11 |
| 12 | 13 | 14 | 15 | 16 | 17 | 18 |
| 19 | 20 | 21 | 22 | 23 | 24 | 25 |
| 26 | 27 | 28 | 29 | 30 |    |    |

### JULY

| MO | TU | WE | TH | FR | SA | SU |
|----|----|----|----|----|----|----|
|    |    |    |    |    | 1  | 2  |
| 3  | 4  | 5  | 6  | 7  | 8  | 9  |
| 10 | 11 | 12 | 13 | 14 | 15 | 16 |
| 17 | 18 | 19 | 20 | 21 | 22 | 23 |
| 24 | 25 | 26 | 27 | 28 | 29 | 30 |
| 31 |    |    |    |    |    |    |

### AUGUST

| MO | TU | WE | TH | FR | SA | SU |
|----|----|----|----|----|----|----|
|    | 1  | 2  | 3  | 4  | 5  | 6  |
| 7  | 8  | 9  | 10 | 11 | 12 | 13 |
| 14 | 15 | 16 | 17 | 18 | 19 | 20 |
| 21 | 22 | 23 | 24 | 25 | 26 | 27 |
| 28 | 29 | 30 | 31 |    |    |    |

### SEPTEMBER

| MO | TU | WE | TH | FR | SA | SU |
|----|----|----|----|----|----|----|
|    |    |    |    | 1  | 2  | 3  |
| 4  | 5  | 6  | 7  | 8  | 9  | 10 |
| 11 | 12 | 13 | 14 | 15 | 16 | 17 |
| 18 | 19 | 20 | 21 | 22 | 23 | 24 |
| 25 | 26 | 27 | 28 | 29 | 30 |    |

### OCTOBER

| MO | TU | WE | TH | FR | SA | SU |
|----|----|----|----|----|----|----|
|    |    |    |    |    |    | 1  |
| 2  | 3  | 4  | 5  | 6  | 7  | 8  |
| 9  | 10 | 11 | 12 | 13 | 14 | 15 |
| 16 | 17 | 18 | 19 | 20 | 21 | 22 |
| 23 | 24 | 25 | 26 | 27 | 28 | 29 |
| 30 | 31 |    |    |    |    |    |

### NOVEMBER

| MO | TU | WE | TH | FR | SA | SU |
|----|----|----|----|----|----|----|
|    |    | 1  | 2  | 3  | 4  | 5  |
| 6  | 7  | 8  | 9  | 10 | 11 | 12 |
| 13 | 14 | 15 | 16 | 17 | 18 | 19 |
| 20 | 21 | 22 | 23 | 24 | 25 | 26 |
| 27 | 28 | 29 | 30 |    |    |    |

### DECEMBER

| MO | TU | WE | TH | FR | SA | SU |
|----|----|----|----|----|----|----|
|    |    |    |    | 1  | 2  | 3  |
| 4  | 5  | 6  | 7  | 8  | 9  | 10 |
| 11 | 12 | 13 | 14 | 15 | 16 | 17 |
| 18 | 19 | 20 | 21 | 22 | 23 | 24 |
| 25 | 26 | 27 | 28 | 29 | 30 | 31 |

# Sample pages

*See it in use!* →

## Annual income TRACKER

|  | AFFILIATE INCOME | AD INCOME | PRODUCT SALES | SPONSORED WORK | OTHER INCOME | TOTAL INCOME | EXPENSES | TOTAL PROFIT |
|---|---|---|---|---|---|---|---|---|
| JAN | $600 | $40 | $2500 | - | $160 | $3,330 | $290 | **$3,010** |

## Blog traffic PROGRESS

|  | BLOG POSTS | MONTHLY SESSIONS | PAGE VIEWS | UNIQUE USERS | TOP TRAFFIC SOURCE | PINTEREST SESSIONS | ORAGANIC SESSIONS | Youtube traffic |
|---|---|---|---|---|---|---|---|---|
| JAN | +7 40 tot | 21,890 | 23,171 | 9,900 | SEO | 4,508 | 12,432 | 709 |

## Audience size TRACKER

|  | ✉ | P | ◉ | 🐦 | f | ▶ | TikTok | TOTAL REACH |
|---|---|---|---|---|---|---|---|---|
| JAN | 5,890 | 40K | 10.4K | 5,6K | 3,K | 620 | 250 | **65.8K** |

**Note:** Do your monthly review sheets first. Then come back to the annual trackers (pages 35-38), and copy the same information, so you can follow your progress throughout the year.

# December
# REVENUE

| AD REVENUE | AMOUNT | DATE |
|---|---|---|
| Media vine payment | $930 | 15 Dec |
| Youtube Ads | $140 | 28 Dec 2022 |
|  |  |  |
|  |  |  |

**TOTAL AD INCOME** — $1,110

# WEEKLY planner

**TO DO:**
- ☐ Publish blog post 1
- ☐ Contact brand
- ☐ Write eBook - chp 5
- ☐
- ☐
- ☐
- ☐
- ☐

**PRIORITIES**

Content creation

FOSUS

# Affiliate programs & payouts
# TRACKER

| NAME | AFFILIATE NETWORK | PAYMENT THRESHOLD | PAYMENT METHOD | EXPECTED PAYOUT DATE | OTHER NOTES |
|---|---|---|---|---|---|
| Etsy | AWIN | $20 | To bank account | -- | Login info on page 3 |
| TSA Courses | Independent | -- | To Paypal | 1st of the month | -- |
| | | | | | |

## PRODUCT #2

**NAME:** Boost Your Blog Traffic eBook

**PRICE:** $25

AFTER 100 SALES, INCREASE THE PRICE BY 10%

**NEW PRICE:** $27.5

**Note:** You can increase your income by increasing your prices. But you want to be justified in doing so. For my digital products, or services I make notes to increase the price when I get x amount of sales or clients. Because then my expertise is worth more! But I always try to offer more value to buyers as well - for example by providing product updates and bonuses.

# Let's talk goals →

# YOUR YEAR AT A GLANCE
## Big plans & goals

JANUARY

FEBRUARY

MARCH

APRIL

MAY

JUNE

JULY

AUGUST

SEPTEMBER

OCTOBER

NOVEMBER

DECEMBER

# narrow down your PRIORITIES

| JANUARY | FEBRUARY | MARCH |
|---|---|---|
| | | |

| APRIL | MAY | JUNE |
|---|---|---|
| | | |

| JULY | AUGUST | SEPTEMBER |
|---|---|---|
| | | |

| OCTOBER | NOVEMBER | DECEMBER |
|---|---|---|
| | | |

# breaking down your income
# GOALS

**THIS YEAR I WANT TO EARN**

**MONTHLY INCOME NEEDED**

Annual income goal % 12 = monthly goal

**AFFILIATE INCOME**

%

**AD INCOME**

%

**DIGITAL PRODUCT SALES**

%

**SPONSORSHIP REVENUE**

%

**SERVICES & FREELANCING**

%

**OTHER INCOME**

%

# *Your annual income goal* TRACKER

**MY GOAL >**

| EARNED | MONTH |
|--------|-------|
|        | DEC   |
|        | NOV   |
|        | OCT   |
|        | SEPT  |
|        | AUG   |
|        | JULY  |
|        | JUN   |
|        | MAY   |
|        | APR   |
|        | MAR   |
|        | FEB   |
|        | JAN   |

SET AN ANNUAL GOAL, AND MILESTONES LEADING UP TO IT.
*Then track your progress every month and colour it in.*

# Blog growth goals

*Write them down!* →

*Plan out your blog growth*
# GOALS

**NR. OF ARTICLES I WANT TO PUBLISH**

**TRAFFIC GOAL FOR THE YEAR**

Page Views

Sessions

**MONTHLY TRAFFIC YOU NEED TO REACH YOUR ANNUAL GOAL**

**EMAIL LIST SIZE**

Page Views per month

Sessions per month

**MAIN TRAFFIC SOURCES**

**SOCIAL MEDIA FOLLOWING**

%

%

*Useful trackers* →

# Blog Content
# TRACKER

| BLOG POST IDEA | CATEGORY | WORD COUNT | OTHER NOTES | DONE |
|---|---|---|---|---|
|  |  |  |  |  |
|  |  |  |  |  |
|  |  |  |  |  |
|  |  |  |  |  |
|  |  |  |  |  |
|  |  |  |  |  |
|  |  |  |  |  |
|  |  |  |  |  |
|  |  |  |  |  |
|  |  |  |  |  |
|  |  |  |  |  |
|  |  |  |  |  |
|  |  |  |  |  |
|  |  |  |  |  |
|  |  |  |  |  |

Category 1:            Category 4:
Category 2:            Category 5:
Category 3:            Category 6:

| BLOG POST IDEA | CATEGORY | WORD COUNT | OTHER NOTES | DONE? |
|---|---|---|---|---|
|  |  |  |  |  |
|  |  |  |  |  |
|  |  |  |  |  |
|  |  |  |  |  |
|  |  |  |  |  |
|  |  |  |  |  |
|  |  |  |  |  |
|  |  |  |  |  |
|  |  |  |  |  |
|  |  |  |  |  |
|  |  |  |  |  |
|  |  |  |  |  |
|  |  |  |  |  |
|  |  |  |  |  |
|  |  |  |  |  |

# Blog Content TRACKER

| BLOG POST IDEA | CATEGORY | WORD COUNT | OTHER NOTES | DONE |
|---|---|---|---|---|
|  |  |  |  |  |
|  |  |  |  |  |
|  |  |  |  |  |
|  |  |  |  |  |
|  |  |  |  |  |
|  |  |  |  |  |
|  |  |  |  |  |
|  |  |  |  |  |
|  |  |  |  |  |
|  |  |  |  |  |
|  |  |  |  |  |
|  |  |  |  |  |
|  |  |  |  |  |

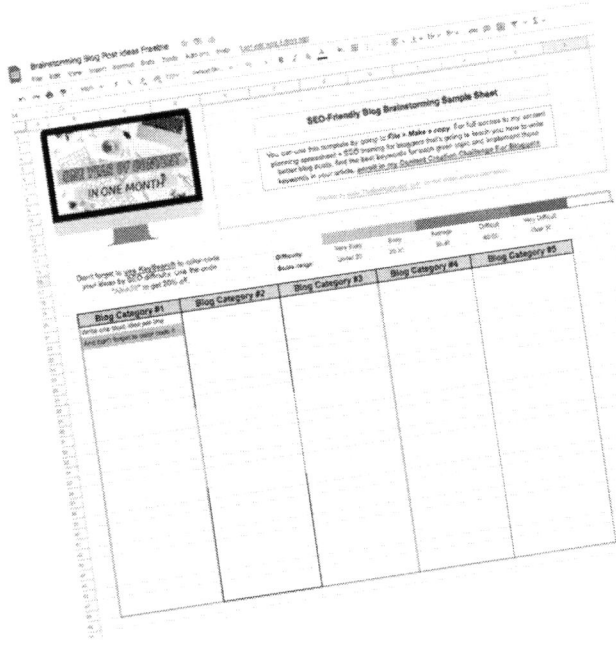

Want a digital blog post tracker and content calendar that you can use online instead?

Grab my "One Year Of Blog Content In One Month Challenge" and get my detailed spreadsheet included.

www.thesheapproach.com/one

Use the code "PLAN30" to get 30% off.

# LOGIN INFO & ACCOUNTS

| ACCOUNT INFO | PASSWORD | NOTES |

| ACCOUNT INFO | PASSWORD | NOTES |

| ACCOUNT INFO | PASSWORD | NOTES |

| ACCOUNT INFO | PASSWORD | NOTES |

| ACCOUNT INFO | PASSWORD | NOTES |

## BANK INFO

## PAYPAL LOGIN

# MORE ACCOUNTS

ACCOUNT INFO					PASSWORD					NOTES


ACCOUNT INFO					PASSWORD					NOTES


ACCOUNT INFO					PASSWORD					NOTES


ACCOUNT INFO					PASSWORD					NOTES


ACCOUNT INFO					PASSWORD					NOTES


## STRIPE LOGIN

# Affiliate programs & payouts TRACKER

| NAME | AFFILIATE NETWORK | PAYMENT THRESHOLD | PAYMENT METHOD | EXPECTED PAYOUT DATE | OTHER NOTES |
|---|---|---|---|---|---|
|  |  |  |  |  |  |
|  |  |  |  |  |  |
|  |  |  |  |  |  |
|  |  |  |  |  |  |
|  |  |  |  |  |  |
|  |  |  |  |  |  |
|  |  |  |  |  |  |
|  |  |  |  |  |  |
|  |  |  |  |  |  |
|  |  |  |  |  |  |
|  |  |  |  |  |  |
|  |  |  |  |  |  |

Affiliate Network 1:

Payout threshold:

Payment method:

Affiliate Network 2:

Payout threshold:

Payment method:

| NAME | AFFILIATE NETWORK | PAYMENT THRESHOLD | PAYMENT METHOD | EXPECTED PAYOUT DATE | OTHER NOTES |
|---|---|---|---|---|---|
|  |  |  |  |  |  |
|  |  |  |  |  |  |
|  |  |  |  |  |  |
|  |  |  |  |  |  |
|  |  |  |  |  |  |
|  |  |  |  |  |  |
|  |  |  |  |  |  |
|  |  |  |  |  |  |
|  |  |  |  |  |  |
|  |  |  |  |  |  |
|  |  |  |  |  |  |
|  |  |  |  |  |  |

# Your prices & offers

*Plan your prices!* →

# PRODUCT #1

NAME:

PRICE:

AFTER [　] SALES, INCREASE THE PRICE BY [　]%

NEW PRICE:

*Notes on how to improve this product or service*

# PRODUCT #2

NAME:

PRICE:

AFTER [ ] SALES, INCREASE THE PRICE BY [ ] %

NEW PRICE:

*Notes on how to improve this product or service*

# PRODUCT #3

NAME:

PRICE:

AFTER [ ] SALES, INCREASE THE PRICE BY [ ] %

NEW PRICE:

*Notes on how to improve this product or service*

# PRODUCT #4

NAME:

PRICE:

AFTER [ ] SALES, INCREASE THE PRICE BY [ ] %

NEW PRICE:

*Notes on how to improve this product or service*

# PRODUCT #5

NAME:

PRICE:

AFTER [ ] SALES, INCREASE THE PRICE BY [ ] %

NEW PRICE:

*Notes on how to improve this product or service*

# VA & FREELANCING SERVICES

*My goal for this year* _____

| PACKAGE | WHAT'S INCLUDED |
|---------|-----------------|
|         |                 |

| PACKAGE | WHAT'S INCLUDED |
|---------|-----------------|
|         |                 |

| PACKAGE | WHAT'S INCLUDED |
|---------|-----------------|
|         |                 |

# WORKING WITH BRANDS

*My goal for this year* _____

| PACKAGE | WHAT'S INCLUDED |
|---------|-----------------|
|         |                 |

| PACKAGE | WHAT'S INCLUDED |
|---------|-----------------|
|         |                 |

| PACKAGE | WHAT'S INCLUDED |
|---------|-----------------|
|         |                 |

# OTHER SERVICES

*My goal for this year* _____

| PACKAGE | WHAT'S INCLUDED |
|---|---|
|  |  |

| PACKAGE | WHAT'S INCLUDED |
|---|---|
|  |  |

| PACKAGE | WHAT'S INCLUDED |
|---|---|
|  |  |

# Annual trackers →

# Annual income
# TRACKER

|  | AFFILIATE INCOME | AD INCOME | PRODUCT SALES | SPONSORED WORK | OTHER INCOME | TOTAL INCOME | EXPENSES | TOTAL PROFIT |
|---|---|---|---|---|---|---|---|---|
| JAN | | | | | | | | |
| FEB | | | | | | | | |
| MAR | | | | | | | | |
| APR | | | | | | | | |
| MAY | | | | | | | | |
| JUN | | | | | | | | |
| JUL | | | | | | | | |
| AUG | | | | | | | | |
| SEPT | | | | | | | | |
| OCT | | | | | | | | |
| NOV | | | | | | | | |
| DEC | | | | | | | | |
| TOTAL | | | | | | | | |

# Blog Traffic PROGRESS

|  | BLOG POSTS | MONTHLY SESSIONS | PAGE VIEWS | UNIQUE USERS | TOP TRAFFIC SOURCE | PINTEREST SESSIONS | ORAGANIC SESSIONS |  |  |
|---|---|---|---|---|---|---|---|---|---|
| JAN |  |  |  |  |  |  |  |  |  |
| FEB |  |  |  |  |  |  |  |  |  |
| MAR |  |  |  |  |  |  |  |  |  |
| APR |  |  |  |  |  |  |  |  |  |
| MAY |  |  |  |  |  |  |  |  |  |
| JUN |  |  |  |  |  |  |  |  |  |
| JUL |  |  |  |  |  |  |  |  |  |
| AUG |  |  |  |  |  |  |  |  |  |
| SEPT |  |  |  |  |  |  |  |  |  |
| OCT |  |  |  |  |  |  |  |  |  |
| NOV |  |  |  |  |  |  |  |  |  |
| DEC |  |  |  |  |  |  |  |  |  |
| TOTAL |  |  |  |  |  |  |  |  |  |

# Audience size TRACKER

|  | ✉ | P | ◎ | 🐦 | f | ▶ |  | TOTAL REACH |
|---|---|---|---|---|---|---|---|---|
| JAN |  |  |  |  |  |  |  |  |
| FEB |  |  |  |  |  |  |  |  |
| MAR |  |  |  |  |  |  |  |  |
| APR |  |  |  |  |  |  |  |  |
| MAY |  |  |  |  |  |  |  |  |
| JUN |  |  |  |  |  |  |  |  |
| JUL |  |  |  |  |  |  |  |  |
| AUG |  |  |  |  |  |  |  |  |
| SEPT |  |  |  |  |  |  |  |  |
| OCT |  |  |  |  |  |  |  |  |
| NOV |  |  |  |  |  |  |  |  |
| DEC |  |  |  |  |  |  |  |  |
| TOTAL |  |  |  |  |  |  |  |  |

# Monthly planner

*Get started!* →

*January* →

MONTH: YEAR:

# JANUARY
*Overview*

| MON | TUE | WED | THU | FRI | SAT | SUN |
|---|---|---|---|---|---|---|
|  |  |  |  |  |  |  |
|  |  |  |  |  |  |  |
|  |  |  |  |  |  |  |
|  |  |  |  |  |  |  |
|  |  |  |  |  |  |  |

Notes: _____
_____
_____
_____
_____

DATES: MONTH: YEAR:

# WEEKLY *planner*

**TO DO:**

○ _____
○ _____
○ _____
○ _____
○ _____
○ _____
○ _____
○ _____
○ _____
○ _____

**PRIORITIES**

*Notes:* _____
_____
_____
_____
_____

DATES: MONTH: YEAR:

# WEEKLY
*planner*

**TO DO:**

- ◯ _____
- ◯ _____
- ◯ _____
- ◯ _____
- ◯ _____
- ◯ _____
- ◯ _____
- ◯ _____
- ◯ _____
- ◯ _____

**PRIORITIES**

*Notes:* _____
_____
_____
_____
_____

DATES:　　　　　MONTH:　　　　　YEAR:

# WEEKLY
*planner*

**TO DO:**

○ _____
○ _____
○ _____
○ _____
○ _____
○ _____
○ _____
○ _____
○ _____
○ _____

**PRIORITIES**

*Notes:* _____
_____
_____
_____
_____

DATES: MONTH: YEAR:

# WEEKLY
*planner*

**TO DO:**

- ○ _____
- ○ _____
- ○ _____
- ○ _____
- ○ _____
- ○ _____
- ○ _____
- ○ _____
- ○ _____
- ○ _____

**PRIORITIES**

*Notes:* _____
_____
_____
_____
_____

# January
# REVENUE

| AFFILIATE SALES | AMOUNT | DATE |
|---|---|---|
|  |  |  |
|  |  |  |
|  |  |  |
|  |  |  |
|  |  |  |
|  |  |  |
|  |  |  |
|  |  |  |
|  |  |  |
|  |  |  |

**TOTAL AFFILIATE INCOME**

| AD REVENUE | AMOUNT | DATE |
|---|---|---|
|  |  |  |
|  |  |  |
|  |  |  |

**TOTAL AD INCOME**

| SERVICES & OFFERS | AMOUNT | DATE |
|---|---|---|
|  |  |  |
|  |  |  |
|  |  |  |
|  |  |  |
|  |  |  |
|  |  |  |
|  |  |  |
|  |  |  |
|  |  |  |
|  |  |  |

**SERVICES INCOME**

| PRODUCT SALES | AMOUNT | DATE |
|---|---|---|
|  |  |  |
|  |  |  |
|  |  |  |
|  |  |  |
|  |  |  |
|  |  |  |
|  |  |  |
|  |  |  |

**TOTAL SALES**

| SPONSORED WORK | AMOUNT | DATE |
|---|---|---|
|  |  |  |
|  |  |  |
|  |  |  |
|  |  |  |
|  |  |  |
|  |  |  |
|  |  |  |
|  |  |  |
|  |  |  |
|  |  |  |

**SPONSORED INCOME**

| OTHER INCOME | AMOUNT | DATE |
|---|---|---|
|  |  |  |
|  |  |  |
|  |  |  |

**ADDITIONAL INCOME**

**TOTAL JANUARY INCOME**

# January EXPENSES

| | EXPENSE | AMOUNT | DATE |
|---|---|---|---|
| | | | |
| | | | |
| | | | |
| | | | |
| | | | |
| | | | |
| | | | |
| | | | |
| | | | |
| | | | |
| | | | |
| | | | |
| | | | |
| | | | |
| | | | |
| | | | |
| | | | |
| | | | |
| | | | |

**TOTAL EXPENSES**

# Your JANUARY review

**PROFIT**

**BIGGEST WIN**

**GOAL**

**ARTICLES**

## BLOG TRAFFIC

| | |
|---|---|
| SESSIONS | |
| PAGE VIEWS | |
| USERS | |
| ORGANIC SESSIONS | |
| PINTEREST SESSIONS | |
| AVR TIME DURATION | |
| | |

## SOCIAL GROWTH

| | STARTING NUMBERS | AT THE END of the month | GROWTH |
|---|---|---|---|
| ✉ | | | |
| Pinterest | | | |
| Twitter | | | |
| Facebook | | | |
| Instagram | | | |
| YouTube | | | |
| | | | |

**TAKEAWAYS**

# MONTHLY
*musings*

### What worked for my blogging business this month

- _____
- _____
- _____
- _____
- _____

## Things to improve

| BLOG CONTENT | TRAFFIC |
|---|---|
|  |  |
| **MARKETING** | **MONETIZATION** |
|  |  |

# February →

MONTH: YEAR:

# FEBRUARY
*Overview*

| MON | TUE | WED | THU | FRI | SAT | SUN |
|-----|-----|-----|-----|-----|-----|-----|
|     |     |     |     |     |     |     |
|     |     |     |     |     |     |     |
|     |     |     |     |     |     |     |
|     |     |     |     |     |     |     |
|     |     |     |     |     |     |     |

*Notes:*

DATES:   MONTH:   YEAR:

# WEEKLY *planner*

**TO DO:**

- ○ _____
- ○ _____
- ○ _____
- ○ _____
- ○ _____
- ○ _____
- ○ _____
- ○ _____
- ○ _____
- ○ _____

**PRIORITIES**

*Notes:* _____

DATES:  MONTH:  YEAR:

# WEEKLY *planner*

**TO DO:**

○ _____
○ _____
○ _____
○ _____
○ _____
○ _____
○ _____
○ _____
○ _____
○ _____

**PRIORITIES**

*Notes:* _____
_____
_____
_____
_____

DATES:   MONTH:   YEAR:

# WEEKLY *planner*

## TO DO:
- ○ _____
- ○ _____
- ○ _____
- ○ _____
- ○ _____
- ○ _____
- ○ _____
- ○ _____
- ○ _____
- ○ _____

## PRIORITIES

*Notes:* _____
_____
_____
_____
_____

DATES: MONTH: YEAR:

# WEEKLY *planner*

**TO DO:**

- ○ _____
- ○ _____
- ○ _____
- ○ _____
- ○ _____
- ○ _____
- ○ _____
- ○ _____
- ○ _____
- ○ _____

**PRIORITIES**

*Notes:* _____
_____
_____
_____
_____

# February REVENUE

| AFFILIATE SALES | AMOUNT | DATE |
|---|---|---|
|  |  |  |
|  |  |  |
|  |  |  |
|  |  |  |
|  |  |  |
|  |  |  |
|  |  |  |
|  |  |  |
|  |  |  |
|  |  |  |

**TOTAL AFFILIATE INCOME**

| AD REVENUE | AMOUNT | DATE |
|---|---|---|
|  |  |  |
|  |  |  |
|  |  |  |

**TOTAL AD INCOME**

| SERVICES & OFFERS | AMOUNT | DATE |
|---|---|---|
|  |  |  |
|  |  |  |
|  |  |  |
|  |  |  |
|  |  |  |
|  |  |  |
|  |  |  |
|  |  |  |
|  |  |  |
|  |  |  |

**SERVICES INCOME**

| PRODUCT SALES | AMOUNT | DATE |
|---|---|---|
|  |  |  |
|  |  |  |
|  |  |  |
|  |  |  |
|  |  |  |
|  |  |  |
|  |  |  |

**TOTAL SALES**

| SPONSORED WORK | AMOUNT | DATE |
|---|---|---|
|  |  |  |
|  |  |  |
|  |  |  |
|  |  |  |
|  |  |  |
|  |  |  |
|  |  |  |
|  |  |  |
|  |  |  |

**SPONSORED INCOME**

| OTHER INCOME | AMOUNT | DATE |
|---|---|---|
|  |  |  |
|  |  |  |
|  |  |  |

**ADDITIONAL INCOME**

**TOTAL FEBRUARY INCOME**

# February EXPENSES

| EXPENSE | AMOUNT | DATE |
|---------|--------|------|
|         |        |      |
|         |        |      |
|         |        |      |
|         |        |      |
|         |        |      |
|         |        |      |
|         |        |      |
|         |        |      |
|         |        |      |
|         |        |      |
|         |        |      |
|         |        |      |
|         |        |      |
|         |        |      |
|         |        |      |
|         |        |      |
|         |        |      |
|         |        |      |

**TOTAL EXPENSES**

# Your FEBRUARY review

## PROFIT

## BIGGEST WIN

## GOAL

## ARTICLES

## BLOG TRAFFIC

| | |
|---|---|
| SESSIONS | |
| PAGE VIEWS | |
| USERS | |
| ORGANIC SESSIONS | |
| PINTEREST SESSIONS | |
| AVR TIME DURATION | |
| | |

## SOCIAL GROWTH

| | STARTING NUMBERS | AT THE END of the month | GROWTH |
|---|---|---|---|
| ✉ | | | |
| P | | | |
| 🐦 | | | |
| f | | | |
| 📷 | | | |
| ▶ | | | |
| | | | |

## TAKEAWAYS

# MONTHLY
*musings*

What worked for my blogging business this month

○ _____
○ _____
○ _____
○ _____
○ _____

*Things to improve*

| BLOG CONTENT | TRAFFIC |
|---|---|
| MARKETING | MONETIZATION |

# March →

MONTH:                                      YEAR:

# MARCH
*Overview*

| MON | TUE | WED | THU | FRI | SAT | SUN |
|-----|-----|-----|-----|-----|-----|-----|
|     |     |     |     |     |     |     |
|     |     |     |     |     |     |     |
|     |     |     |     |     |     |     |
|     |     |     |     |     |     |     |
|     |     |     |     |     |     |     |

*Notes:* _____
_____
_____
_____
_____

DATES: MONTH: YEAR:

# WEEKLY *planner*

**TO DO:**

- ○ _____
- ○ _____
- ○ _____
- ○ _____
- ○ _____
- ○ _____
- ○ _____
- ○ _____
- ○ _____
- ○ _____

**PRIORITIES**

*Notes:* _____
_____
_____
_____
_____

DATES:　　　　　　MONTH:　　　　　　YEAR:

# WEEKLY
*planner*

**TO DO:**

- ○ _____
- ○ _____
- ○ _____
- ○ _____
- ○ _____
- ○ _____
- ○ _____
- ○ _____
- ○ _____
- ○ _____

**PRIORITIES**

*Notes:* _____

DATES: MONTH: YEAR:

# WEEKLY *planner*

**TO DO:**

- ○ _____
- ○ _____
- ○ _____
- ○ _____
- ○ _____
- ○ _____
- ○ _____
- ○ _____
- ○ _____
- ○ _____

**PRIORITIES**

*Notes:* _____
_____
_____
_____

DATES: MONTH: YEAR:

# WEEKLY
*planner*

**TO DO:**

- ○ _____
- ○ _____
- ○ _____
- ○ _____
- ○ _____
- ○ _____
- ○ _____
- ○ _____
- ○ _____
- ○ _____

**PRIORITIES**

*Notes:* _____
_____
_____
_____

# March
# REVENUE

| AFFILIATE SALES | AMOUNT | DATE | |
|---|---|---|---|
| | | | |
| | | | |
| | | | |
| | | | |
| | | | |
| | | | |
| | | | |
| | | | |
| | | | |
| | | | |

**TOTAL AFFILIATE INCOME**

| AD REVENUE | AMOUNT | DATE | |
|---|---|---|---|
| | | | |
| | | | |
| | | | |

**TOTAL AD INCOME**

| SERVICES & OFFERS | AMOUNT | DATE |
|---|---|---|
|  |  |  |
|  |  |  |
|  |  |  |
|  |  |  |
|  |  |  |
|  |  |  |
|  |  |  |
|  |  |  |
|  |  |  |
|  |  |  |

**SERVICES INCOME**

| PRODUCT SALES | AMOUNT | DATE |
|---|---|---|
|  |  |  |
|  |  |  |
|  |  |  |
|  |  |  |
|  |  |  |
|  |  |  |
|  |  |  |

**TOTAL SALES**

| SPONSORED WORK | AMOUNT | DATE |
|---|---|---|
|  |  |  |
|  |  |  |
|  |  |  |
|  |  |  |
|  |  |  |
|  |  |  |
|  |  |  |
|  |  |  |
|  |  |  |

**SPONSORED INCOME**

| OTHER INCOME | AMOUNT | DATE |
|---|---|---|
|  |  |  |
|  |  |  |
|  |  |  |

**ADDITIONAL INCOME**

**TOTAL MARCH INCOME**

# March
# EXPENSES

| EXPENSE | AMOUNT | DATE |
|---|---|---|
|  |  |  |
|  |  |  |
|  |  |  |
|  |  |  |
|  |  |  |
|  |  |  |
|  |  |  |
|  |  |  |
|  |  |  |
|  |  |  |
|  |  |  |
|  |  |  |
|  |  |  |
|  |  |  |
|  |  |  |
|  |  |  |
|  |  |  |

**TOTAL EXPENSES**

# Your **MARCH** review

## PROFIT

### BIGGEST WIN

## BLOG TRAFFIC

| | |
|---|---|
| SESSIONS | |
| PAGE VIEWS | |
| USERS | |
| ORGANIC SESSIONS | |
| PINTEREST SESSIONS | |
| AVR TIME DURATION | |
| | |

## GOAL

## ARTICLES

## SOCIAL GROWTH

| | STARTING NUMBERS | AT THE END of the month | GROWTH |
|---|---|---|---|
| ✉ | | | |
| P | | | |
| 🐦 | | | |
| f | | | |
| 📷 | | | |
| ▶ | | | |
| | | | |

## TAKEAWAYS

# MONTHLY
*musings*

### What worked for my blogging business this month

- _____
- _____
- _____
- _____
- _____

## Things to improve

| BLOG CONTENT | TRAFFIC |
|---|---|
| MARKETING | MONETIZATION |

*April* →

MONTH: YEAR:

# APRIL
## Overview

| MON | TUE | WED | THU | FRI | SAT | SUN |
|-----|-----|-----|-----|-----|-----|-----|
|     |     |     |     |     |     |     |
|     |     |     |     |     |     |     |
|     |     |     |     |     |     |     |
|     |     |     |     |     |     |     |
|     |     |     |     |     |     |     |

Notes: _____
_____
_____
_____

DATES: MONTH: YEAR:

# WEEKLY *planner*

**TO DO:**

- ○ _____
- ○ _____
- ○ _____
- ○ _____
- ○ _____
- ○ _____
- ○ _____
- ○ _____
- ○ _____
- ○ _____

**PRIORITIES**

*Notes:* _____

DATES:　　　　　　　MONTH:　　　　　　　YEAR:

# WEEKLY *planner*

**TO DO:**
- ○ _____
- ○ _____
- ○ _____
- ○ _____
- ○ _____
- ○ _____
- ○ _____
- ○ _____
- ○ _____
- ○ _____

**PRIORITIES**

*Notes:* _____

# April REVENUE

| AFFILIATE SALES | AMOUNT | DATE |
|---|---|---|
| | | |
| | | |
| | | |
| | | |
| | | |
| | | |
| | | |
| | | |
| | | |
| | | |

**TOTAL AFFILIATE INCOME**

| AD REVENUE | AMOUNT | DATE |
|---|---|---|
| | | |
| | | |
| | | |
| | | |

**TOTAL AD INCOME**

| SERVICES & OFFERS | AMOUNT | DATE |
|---|---|---|
|  |  |  |
|  |  |  |
|  |  |  |
|  |  |  |
|  |  |  |
|  |  |  |
|  |  |  |
|  |  |  |
|  |  |  |
|  |  |  |

**SERVICES INCOME**

| PRODUCT SALES | AMOUNT | DATE |
|---|---|---|
|  |  |  |
|  |  |  |
|  |  |  |
|  |  |  |
|  |  |  |
|  |  |  |
|  |  |  |

**TOTAL SALES**

| SPONSORED WORK | AMOUNT | DATE |
|---|---|---|
|  |  |  |
|  |  |  |
|  |  |  |
|  |  |  |
|  |  |  |
|  |  |  |
|  |  |  |
|  |  |  |
|  |  |  |
|  |  |  |

**SPONSORED INCOME**

| OTHER INCOME | AMOUNT | DATE |
|---|---|---|
|  |  |  |
|  |  |  |
|  |  |  |

**ADDITIONAL INCOME**

**TOTAL APRIL INCOME**

# April
# EXPENSES

| EXPENSE | AMOUNT | DATE |
|---------|--------|------|
|         |        |      |
|         |        |      |
|         |        |      |
|         |        |      |
|         |        |      |
|         |        |      |
|         |        |      |
|         |        |      |
|         |        |      |
|         |        |      |
|         |        |      |
|         |        |      |
|         |        |      |
|         |        |      |
|         |        |      |
|         |        |      |
|         |        |      |
|         |        |      |
|         |        |      |

**TOTAL EXPENSES**

# Your **APRIL** review

## PROFIT

### BIGGEST WIN

## BLOG TRAFFIC

| | |
|---|---|
| SESSIONS | |
| PAGE VIEWS | |
| USERS | |
| ORGANIC SESSIONS | |
| PINTEREST SESSIONS | |
| AVR TIME DURATION | |
| | |

## GOAL

## ARTICLES

## SOCIAL GROWTH

| | STARTING NUMBERS | AT THE END of the month | GROWTH |
|---|---|---|---|
| ✉ | | | |
| P | | | |
| 🐦 | | | |
| f | | | |
| 📷 | | | |
| ▶ | | | |
| | | | |

## TAKEAWAYS

# MONTHLY
*musings*

What worked for my blogging business this month

○ _____
○ _____
○ _____
○ _____
○ _____

*Things to improve*

| BLOG CONTENT | TRAFFIC |
|---|---|
| | |
| MARKETING | MONETIZATION |
| | |

*May* →

MONTH: YEAR:

# MAY
## Overview

| MON | TUE | WED | THU | FRI | SAT | SUN |
|---|---|---|---|---|---|---|
|  |  |  |  |  |  |  |
|  |  |  |  |  |  |  |
|  |  |  |  |  |  |  |
|  |  |  |  |  |  |  |
|  |  |  |  |  |  |  |

Notes:

DATES: MONTH: YEAR:

# WEEKLY *planner*

**TO DO:**

○ _____
○ _____
○ _____
○ _____
○ _____
○ _____
○ _____
○ _____
○ _____
○ _____

**PRIORITIES**

*Notes:* _____
_____
_____
_____
_____

DATES: MONTH: YEAR:

# WEEKLY *planner*

**TO DO:**

○ _____
○ _____
○ _____
○ _____
○ _____
○ _____
○ _____
○ _____
○ _____
○ _____

**PRIORITIES**

*Notes:* _____
_____
_____
_____
_____

DATES:　　　　　　MONTH:　　　　　　YEAR:

# WEEKLY *planner*

**TO DO:**
- ○ _____
- ○ _____
- ○ _____
- ○ _____
- ○ _____
- ○ _____
- ○ _____
- ○ _____
- ○ _____
- ○ _____

**PRIORITIES**

*Notes:* _____

DATES: MONTH: YEAR:

# WEEKLY
*planner*

**TO DO:**

○ _____
○ _____
○ _____
○ _____
○ _____
○ _____
○ _____
○ _____
○ _____
○ _____

**PRIORITIES**

*Notes:* _____
_____
_____
_____
_____

| AFFILIATE SALES | AMOUNT | DATE |
|---|---|---|
|  |  |  |
|  |  |  |
|  |  |  |
|  |  |  |
|  |  |  |
|  |  |  |
|  |  |  |
|  |  |  |
|  |  |  |
|  |  |  |

**TOTAL AFFILIATE INCOME**

| AD REVENUE | AMOUNT | DATE |
|---|---|---|
|  |  |  |
|  |  |  |
|  |  |  |

**TOTAL AD INCOME**

| SERVICES & OFFERS | AMOUNT | DATE |
|---|---|---|
|  |  |  |
|  |  |  |
|  |  |  |
|  |  |  |
|  |  |  |
|  |  |  |
|  |  |  |
|  |  |  |
|  |  |  |
|  |  |  |
|  |  |  |
|  |  |  |

**SERVICES INCOME**

| PRODUCT SALES | AMOUNT | DATE |
|---|---|---|
|  |  |  |
|  |  |  |
|  |  |  |
|  |  |  |
|  |  |  |
|  |  |  |
|  |  |  |
|  |  |  |

**TOTAL SALES**

| SPONSORED WORK | AMOUNT | DATE |
|---|---|---|
| | | |
| | | |
| | | |
| | | |
| | | |
| | | |
| | | |
| | | |
| | | |
| | | |

**SPONSORED INCOME**

| OTHER INCOME | AMOUNT | DATE |
|---|---|---|
| | | |
| | | |
| | | |
| | | |

**ADDITIONAL INCOME**

**TOTAL MAY INCOME**

# May EXPENSES

| EXPENSE | AMOUNT | DATE |
|---------|--------|------|
|         |        |      |
|         |        |      |
|         |        |      |
|         |        |      |
|         |        |      |
|         |        |      |
|         |        |      |
|         |        |      |
|         |        |      |
|         |        |      |
|         |        |      |
|         |        |      |
|         |        |      |
|         |        |      |
|         |        |      |
|         |        |      |
|         |        |      |
|         |        |      |

**TOTAL EXPENSES**

# Your  review

## PROFIT

## BIGGEST WIN

## GOAL

## ARTICLES

## BLOG TRAFFIC

| | |
|---|---|
| SESSIONS | |
| PAGE VIEWS | |
| USERS | |
| ORGANIC SESSIONS | |
| PINTEREST SESSIONS | |
| AVR TIME DURATION | |
| | |

## SOCIAL GROWTH

| | STARTING NUMBERS | AT THE END of the month | GROWTH |
|---|---|---|---|
| ✉ | | | |
| P | | | |
| 🐦 | | | |
| f | | | |
| 📷 | | | |
| ▶ | | | |
| | | | |

## TAKEAWAYS

# MONTHLY
*musings*

What worked for my blogging business this month

○ _____
○ _____
○ _____
○ _____
○ _____

*Things to improve*

| BLOG CONTENT | TRAFFIC |
| --- | --- |
| MARKETING | MONETIZATION |

# Notes

# June →

MONTH: YEAR:

# JUNE
*Overview*

| MON | TUE | WED | THU | FRI | SAT | SUN |
|---|---|---|---|---|---|---|
|  |  |  |  |  |  |  |
|  |  |  |  |  |  |  |
|  |  |  |  |  |  |  |
|  |  |  |  |  |  |  |
|  |  |  |  |  |  |  |

*Notes:* _____
_____
_____
_____

DATES: MONTH: YEAR:

# WEEKLY
*planner*

## TO DO:
○ _____
○ _____
○ _____
○ _____
○ _____
○ _____
○ _____
○ _____
○ _____
○ _____

## PRIORITIES

*Notes:* _____
_____
_____
_____

DATES:　　　　　MONTH:　　　　　YEAR:

# WEEKLY *planner*

**TO DO:**

- ○ _____
- ○ _____
- ○ _____
- ○ _____
- ○ _____
- ○ _____
- ○ _____
- ○ _____
- ○ _____
- ○ _____

**PRIORITIES**

*Notes:* _____

DATES: MONTH: YEAR:

# WEEKLY *planner*

**TO DO:**
- ○ _____
- ○ _____
- ○ _____
- ○ _____
- ○ _____
- ○ _____
- ○ _____
- ○ _____
- ○ _____
- ○ _____

**PRIORITIES**

*Notes:* _____
_____
_____
_____

DATES:  MONTH:  YEAR:

# WEEKLY *planner*

**TO DO:**

- ○ _____
- ○ _____
- ○ _____
- ○ _____
- ○ _____
- ○ _____
- ○ _____
- ○ _____
- ○ _____
- ○ _____

**PRIORITIES**

*Notes:* _____
_____
_____
_____

# June
# REVENUE

| AFFILIATE SALES | AMOUNT | DATE |
|---|---|---|
| | | |
| | | |
| | | |
| | | |
| | | |
| | | |
| | | |
| | | |
| | | |
| | | |
| | | |

**TOTAL AFFILIATE INCOME**

| AD REVENUE | AMOUNT | DATE |
|---|---|---|
| | | |
| | | |
| | | |

**TOTAL AD INCOME**

| SERVICES & OFFERS | AMOUNT | DATE |
|---|---|---|
|  |  |  |
|  |  |  |
|  |  |  |
|  |  |  |
|  |  |  |
|  |  |  |
|  |  |  |
|  |  |  |
|  |  |  |
|  |  |  |

**SERVICES INCOME**

| PRODUCT SALES | AMOUNT | DATE |
|---|---|---|
|  |  |  |
|  |  |  |
|  |  |  |
|  |  |  |
|  |  |  |
|  |  |  |
|  |  |  |

**TOTAL SALES**

| SPONSORED WORK | AMOUNT | DATE |
|---|---|---|
|  |  |  |
|  |  |  |
|  |  |  |
|  |  |  |
|  |  |  |
|  |  |  |
|  |  |  |
|  |  |  |
|  |  |  |
|  |  |  |
|  |  |  |
|  |  |  |

**SPONSORED INCOME**

| OTHER INCOME | AMOUNT | DATE |
|---|---|---|
|  |  |  |
|  |  |  |
|  |  |  |

**ADDITIONAL INCOME**

**TOTAL JUNE INCOME**

# *June* EXPENSES

| EXPENSE | AMOUNT | DATE | |
|---|---|---|---|
|  |  |  |  |
|  |  |  |  |
|  |  |  |  |
|  |  |  |  |
|  |  |  |  |
|  |  |  |  |
|  |  |  |  |
|  |  |  |  |
|  |  |  |  |
|  |  |  |  |
|  |  |  |  |
|  |  |  |  |
|  |  |  |  |
|  |  |  |  |
|  |  |  |  |
|  |  |  |  |
|  |  |  |  |
|  |  |  |  |
|  |  |  |  |

**TOTAL EXPENSES**

# Your **JUNE** review

## PROFIT

## BIGGEST WIN

## GOAL

## ARTICLES

## BLOG TRAFFIC

| | |
|---|---|
| SESSIONS | |
| PAGE VIEWS | |
| USERS | |
| ORGANIC SESSIONS | |
| PINTEREST SESSIONS | |
| AVR TIME DURATION | |
| | |

## SOCIAL GROWTH

| | STARTING NUMBERS | AT THE END of the month | GROWTH |
|---|---|---|---|
| ✉ | | | |
| P | | | |
| 🐦 | | | |
| f | | | |
| 📷 | | | |
| ▶ | | | |
| | | | |

## TAKEAWAYS

# MONTHLY
*musings*

### What worked for my blogging business this month

○ _____
○ _____
○ _____
○ _____
○ _____

## Things to improve

| BLOG CONTENT | TRAFFIC |
|---|---|
|  |  |
| **MARKETING** | **MONETIZATION** |
|  |  |

# July →

MONTH: YEAR:

# JULY
*Overview*

| MON | TUE | WED | THU | FRI | SAT | SUN |
|---|---|---|---|---|---|---|
| | | | | | | |
| | | | | | | |
| | | | | | | |
| | | | | | | |
| | | | | | | |

*Notes:* _____
_____
_____
_____
_____

DATES: MONTH: YEAR:

# WEEKLY
*planner*

**TO DO:**
- ○ _____
- ○ _____
- ○ _____
- ○ _____
- ○ _____
- ○ _____
- ○ _____
- ○ _____
- ○ _____
- ○ _____

**PRIORITIES**

*Notes:* _____
_____
_____
_____
_____

DATES: MONTH: YEAR:

# WEEKLY *planner*

**TO DO:**

- ○ _____
- ○ _____
- ○ _____
- ○ _____
- ○ _____
- ○ _____
- ○ _____
- ○ _____
- ○ _____
- ○ _____

**PRIORITIES**

*Notes:* _____
_____
_____
_____

DATES:  MONTH:  YEAR:

# WEEKLY
*planner*

## TO DO:
- ○ _____
- ○ _____
- ○ _____
- ○ _____
- ○ _____
- ○ _____
- ○ _____
- ○ _____
- ○ _____
- ○ _____

## PRIORITIES

*Notes:* _____

DATES:  MONTH:  YEAR:

# WEEKLY *planner*

**TO DO:**

○ _____
○ _____
○ _____
○ _____
○ _____
○ _____
○ _____
○ _____
○ _____
○ _____

**PRIORITIES**

*Notes:* _____
_____
_____
_____

| AFFILIATE SALES | AMOUNT | DATE |
|---|---|---|
|  |  |  |
|  |  |  |
|  |  |  |
|  |  |  |
|  |  |  |
|  |  |  |
|  |  |  |
|  |  |  |
|  |  |  |
|  |  |  |

**TOTAL AFFILIATE INCOME**

| AD REVENUE | AMOUNT | DATE |
|---|---|---|
|  |  |  |
|  |  |  |
|  |  |  |
|  |  |  |

**TOTAL AD INCOME**

| SERVICES & OFFERS | AMOUNT | DATE | |
|---|---|---|---|
| | | | |
| | | | |
| | | | |
| | | | |
| | | | |
| | | | |
| | | | |
| | | | |
| | | | |
| | | | |
| | | | |
| | | | |
| | | | |

**SERVICES INCOME**

| PRODUCT SALES | AMOUNT | DATE | |
|---|---|---|---|
| | | | |
| | | | |
| | | | |
| | | | |
| | | | |
| | | | |
| | | | |

**TOTAL SALES**

| SPONSORED WORK | AMOUNT | DATE |
|---|---|---|
|  |  |  |
|  |  |  |
|  |  |  |
|  |  |  |
|  |  |  |
|  |  |  |
|  |  |  |
|  |  |  |
|  |  |  |
|  |  |  |

**SPONSORED INCOME**

| OTHER INCOME | AMOUNT | DATE |
|---|---|---|
|  |  |  |
|  |  |  |
|  |  |  |

**ADDITIONAL INCOME**

**TOTAL JULY INCOME**

# *July* EXPENSES

| EXPENSE | AMOUNT | DATE |
|---|---|---|
|  |  |  |
|  |  |  |
|  |  |  |
|  |  |  |
|  |  |  |
|  |  |  |
|  |  |  |
|  |  |  |
|  |  |  |
|  |  |  |
|  |  |  |
|  |  |  |
|  |  |  |
|  |  |  |
|  |  |  |
|  |  |  |
|  |  |  |
|  |  |  |
|  |  |  |
|  |  |  |

**TOTAL EXPENSES**

# Your JULY review

## PROFIT

## BIGGEST WIN

## GOAL

## ARTICLES

## BLOG TRAFFIC

| | |
|---|---|
| SESSIONS | |
| PAGE VIEWS | |
| USERS | |
| ORGANIC SESSIONS | |
| PINTEREST SESSIONS | |
| AVR TIME DURATION | |

## SOCIAL GROWTH

| | STARTING NUMBERS | AT THE END of the month | GROWTH |
|---|---|---|---|
| ✉ | | | |
| P | | | |
| 🐦 | | | |
| f | | | |
| 📷 | | | |
| ▶ | | | |

## TAKEAWAYS

# MONTHLY
*musings*

What worked for my blogging business this month

- ○ _____
- ○ _____
- ○ _____
- ○ _____
- ○ _____

*Things to improve*

| BLOG CONTENT | TRAFFIC |
|---|---|
| MARKETING | MONETIZATION |

# August →

MONTH: YEAR:

# AUGUST
## Overview

| MON | TUE | WED | THU | FRI | SAT | SUN |
|-----|-----|-----|-----|-----|-----|-----|
|     |     |     |     |     |     |     |
|     |     |     |     |     |     |     |
|     |     |     |     |     |     |     |
|     |     |     |     |     |     |     |
|     |     |     |     |     |     |     |

Notes: _____
_____
_____
_____
_____

DATES: MONTH: YEAR:

# WEEKLY *planner*

**TO DO:**
- ○ _____
- ○ _____
- ○ _____
- ○ _____
- ○ _____
- ○ _____
- ○ _____
- ○ _____
- ○ _____
- ○ _____

**PRIORITIES**

*Notes:* _____
_____
_____
_____
_____

DATES:　　　　　　　MONTH:　　　　　　　YEAR:

# WEEKLY
*planner*

**TO DO:**

○ _____
○ _____
○ _____
○ _____
○ _____
○ _____
○ _____
○ _____
○ _____
○ _____

**PRIORITIES**

*Notes:* _____

DATES:  MONTH:  YEAR:

# WEEKLY *planner*

## TO DO:

○ _____
○ _____
○ _____
○ _____
○ _____
○ _____
○ _____
○ _____
○ _____
○ _____

## PRIORITIES

*Notes:* _____
_____
_____
_____

DATES:　　　　　MONTH:　　　　　YEAR:

# WEEKLY *planner*

**TO DO:**

- ○ _____
- ○ _____
- ○ _____
- ○ _____
- ○ _____
- ○ _____
- ○ _____
- ○ _____
- ○ _____
- ○ _____

**PRIORITIES**

*Notes:* _____
_____
_____
_____

# August REVENUE

| AFFILIATE SALES | AMOUNT | DATE |
|---|---|---|
| | | |
| | | |
| | | |
| | | |
| | | |
| | | |
| | | |
| | | |
| | | |
| | | |
| | | |

**TOTAL AFFILIATE INCOME**

| AD REVENUE | AMOUNT | DATE |
|---|---|---|
| | | |
| | | |
| | | |

**TOTAL AD INCOME**

| SERVICES & OFFERS | AMOUNT | DATE | |
|---|---|---|---|
| | | | |
| | | | |
| | | | |
| | | | |
| | | | |
| | | | |
| | | | |
| | | | |
| | | | |
| | | | |

## SERVICES INCOME

| PRODUCT SALES | AMOUNT | DATE | |
|---|---|---|---|
| | | | |
| | | | |
| | | | |
| | | | |
| | | | |
| | | | |
| | | | |

## TOTAL SALES

| SPONSORED WORK | AMOUNT | DATE |
|---|---|---|
| | | |
| | | |
| | | |
| | | |
| | | |
| | | |
| | | |
| | | |
| | | |
| | | |

**SPONSORED INCOME**

| OTHER INCOME | AMOUNT | DATE |
|---|---|---|
| | | |
| | | |
| | | |

**ADDITIONAL INCOME**

**TOTAL AUGUST INCOME**

# August EXPENSES

| EXPENSE | AMOUNT | DATE |
|---------|--------|------|
|         |        |      |
|         |        |      |
|         |        |      |
|         |        |      |
|         |        |      |
|         |        |      |
|         |        |      |
|         |        |      |
|         |        |      |
|         |        |      |
|         |        |      |
|         |        |      |
|         |        |      |
|         |        |      |
|         |        |      |
|         |        |      |
|         |        |      |

**TOTAL EXPENSES**

# Your **AUGUST** review

**PROFIT**

**BIGGEST WIN**

**BLOG TRAFFIC**

| | |
|---|---|
| SESSIONS | |
| PAGE VIEWS | |
| USERS | |
| ORGANIC SESSIONS | |
| PINTEREST SESSIONS | |
| AVR TIME DURATION | |
| | |

**GOAL**

**ARTICLES**

**SOCIAL GROWTH**

| | STARTING NUMBERS | AT THE END of the month | GROWTH |
|---|---|---|---|
| ✉ | | | |
| P | | | |
| 🐦 | | | |
| f | | | |
| 📷 | | | |
| ▶ | | | |
| | | | |

**TAKEAWAYS**

# MONTHLY
*musings*

### What worked for my blogging business this month

- _____
- _____
- _____
- _____
- _____

## Things to improve

| BLOG CONTENT | TRAFFIC |
|---|---|
|  |  |
| MARKETING | MONETIZATION |
|  |  |

# September →

MONTH: YEAR:

# SEPTEMBER
## *Overview*

| MON | TUE | WED | THU | FRI | SAT | SUN |
|-----|-----|-----|-----|-----|-----|-----|
|     |     |     |     |     |     |     |
|     |     |     |     |     |     |     |
|     |     |     |     |     |     |     |
|     |     |     |     |     |     |     |
|     |     |     |     |     |     |     |

Notes:
_____
_____
_____
_____

DATES: MONTH: YEAR:

# WEEKLY *planner*

**TO DO:**
- ○ _____
- ○ _____
- ○ _____
- ○ _____
- ○ _____
- ○ _____
- ○ _____
- ○ _____
- ○ _____
- ○ _____

**PRIORITIES**

*Notes:* _____

DATES: MONTH: YEAR:

# WEEKLY *planner*

**TO DO:**

- ○ _____
- ○ _____
- ○ _____
- ○ _____
- ○ _____
- ○ _____
- ○ _____
- ○ _____
- ○ _____
- ○ _____

**PRIORITIES**

*Notes:* _____
_____
_____
_____

DATES: MONTH: YEAR:

# WEEKLY *planner*

**TO DO:**

- ○ _____
- ○ _____
- ○ _____
- ○ _____
- ○ _____
- ○ _____
- ○ _____
- ○ _____
- ○ _____
- ○ _____

**PRIORITIES**

*Notes:* _____
_____
_____
_____
_____

DATES: MONTH: YEAR:

# WEEKLY *planner*

**TO DO:**

- ○ _____
- ○ _____
- ○ _____
- ○ _____
- ○ _____
- ○ _____
- ○ _____
- ○ _____
- ○ _____
- ○ _____

**PRIORITIES**

*Notes:* _____
_____
_____
_____

# September
# REVENUE

| AFFILIATE SALES | AMOUNT | DATE |
|---|---|---|
|  |  |  |
|  |  |  |
|  |  |  |
|  |  |  |
|  |  |  |
|  |  |  |
|  |  |  |
|  |  |  |
|  |  |  |
|  |  |  |

**TOTAL AFFILIATE INCOME**

| AD REVENUE | AMOUNT | DATE |
|---|---|---|
|  |  |  |
|  |  |  |
|  |  |  |
|  |  |  |

**TOTAL AD INCOME**

| SERVICES & OFFERS | AMOUNT | DATE |
|---|---|---|
|  |  |  |
|  |  |  |
|  |  |  |
|  |  |  |
|  |  |  |
|  |  |  |
|  |  |  |
|  |  |  |
|  |  |  |
|  |  |  |
|  |  |  |
|  |  |  |

**SERVICES INCOME**

| PRODUCT SALES | AMOUNT | DATE |
|---|---|---|
|  |  |  |
|  |  |  |
|  |  |  |
|  |  |  |
|  |  |  |
|  |  |  |
|  |  |  |
|  |  |  |

**TOTAL SALES**

| SPONSORED WORK | AMOUNT | DATE |
|---|---|---|
|  |  |  |
|  |  |  |
|  |  |  |
|  |  |  |
|  |  |  |
|  |  |  |
|  |  |  |
|  |  |  |
|  |  |  |
|  |  |  |

**SPONSORED INCOME**

| OTHER INCOME | AMOUNT | DATE |
|---|---|---|
|  |  |  |
|  |  |  |
|  |  |  |

**ADDITIONAL INCOME**

**TOTAL SEPTEMBER INCOME**

# September
# EXPENSES

| EXPENSE | AMOUNT | DATE |
|---------|--------|------|
|         |        |      |
|         |        |      |
|         |        |      |
|         |        |      |
|         |        |      |
|         |        |      |
|         |        |      |
|         |        |      |
|         |        |      |
|         |        |      |
|         |        |      |
|         |        |      |
|         |        |      |
|         |        |      |
|         |        |      |
|         |        |      |
|         |        |      |
|         |        |      |
|         |        |      |
|         |        |      |

**TOTAL EXPENSES**

# Your SEPTEMBER review

**PROFIT**

**BIGGEST WIN**

**GOAL**

**ARTICLES**

## BLOG TRAFFIC

| | |
|---|---|
| SESSIONS | |
| PAGE VIEWS | |
| USERS | |
| ORGANIC SESSIONS | |
| PINTEREST SESSIONS | |
| AVR TIME DURATION | |

## SOCIAL GROWTH

| | STARTING NUMBERS | AT THE END of the month | GROWTH |
|---|---|---|---|
| ✉ | | | |
| P | | | |
| 🐦 | | | |
| f | | | |
| 📷 | | | |
| ▶ | | | |
| | | | |

**TAKEAWAYS**

# MONTHLY
*musings*

### What worked for my blogging business this month

○ _____
○ _____
○ _____
○ _____
○ _____

## Things to improve

| BLOG CONTENT | TRAFFIC |
| --- | --- |
| MARKETING | MONETIZATION |

# October →

MONTH: YEAR:

# OCTOBER
*Overview*

| MON | TUE | WED | THU | FRI | SAT | SUN |
|---|---|---|---|---|---|---|
|  |  |  |  |  |  |  |
|  |  |  |  |  |  |  |
|  |  |  |  |  |  |  |
|  |  |  |  |  |  |  |
|  |  |  |  |  |  |  |

*Notes:* _____
_____
_____
_____

DATES: MONTH: YEAR:

# WEEKLY
*planner*

**TO DO:**

○ _____

○ _____

○ _____

○ _____

○ _____

○ _____

○ _____

○ _____

○ _____

○ _____

**PRIORITIES**

*Notes:* _____
_____
_____
_____

DATES: MONTH: YEAR:

# WEEKLY
*planner*

**TO DO:**

- ○ _____
- ○ _____
- ○ _____
- ○ _____
- ○ _____
- ○ _____
- ○ _____
- ○ _____
- ○ _____
- ○ _____

**PRIORITIES**

*Notes:* _____
_____
_____
_____
_____

DATES:　　　　　　　MONTH:　　　　　　　YEAR:

# WEEKLY *planner*

**TO DO:**

- ○ _____
- ○ _____
- ○ _____
- ○ _____
- ○ _____
- ○ _____
- ○ _____
- ○ _____
- ○ _____
- ○ _____

**PRIORITIES**

*Notes:* _____
_____
_____
_____

| SERVICES & OFFERS | AMOUNT | DATE |
|---|---|---|
|  |  |  |
|  |  |  |
|  |  |  |
|  |  |  |
|  |  |  |
|  |  |  |
|  |  |  |
|  |  |  |
|  |  |  |
|  |  |  |

**SERVICES INCOME**

| PRODUCT SALES | AMOUNT | DATE |
|---|---|---|
|  |  |  |
|  |  |  |
|  |  |  |
|  |  |  |
|  |  |  |
|  |  |  |
|  |  |  |

**TOTAL SALES**

| SPONSORED WORK | AMOUNT | DATE |
|---|---|---|
|  |  |  |
|  |  |  |
|  |  |  |
|  |  |  |
|  |  |  |
|  |  |  |
|  |  |  |
|  |  |  |
|  |  |  |
|  |  |  |

**SPONSORED INCOME**

| OTHER INCOME | AMOUNT | DATE |
|---|---|---|
|  |  |  |
|  |  |  |
|  |  |  |
|  |  |  |

**ADDITIONAL INCOME**

**TOTAL OCTOBER INCOME**

# *October* EXPENSES

| EXPENSE | AMOUNT | DATE |
|---------|--------|------|
|         |        |      |
|         |        |      |
|         |        |      |
|         |        |      |
|         |        |      |
|         |        |      |
|         |        |      |
|         |        |      |
|         |        |      |
|         |        |      |
|         |        |      |
|         |        |      |
|         |        |      |
|         |        |      |
|         |        |      |
|         |        |      |
|         |        |      |
|         |        |      |
|         |        |      |
|         |        |      |

**TOTAL EXPENSES**

# Your OCTOBER review

**PROFIT**

**BIGGEST WIN**

**GOAL**

**ARTICLES**

## BLOG TRAFFIC

| | |
|---|---|
| SESSIONS | |
| PAGE VIEWS | |
| USERS | |
| ORGANIC SESSIONS | |
| PINTEREST SESSIONS | |
| AVR TIME DURATION | |

## SOCIAL GROWTH

| | STARTING NUMBERS | AT THE END of the month | GROWTH |
|---|---|---|---|
| ✉ | | | |
| P | | | |
| 🐦 | | | |
| f | | | |
| 📷 | | | |
| ▶ | | | |
| | | | |

**TAKEAWAYS**

# MONTHLY
*musings*

### What worked for my blogging business this month

○ _____
○ _____
○ _____
○ _____
○ _____

## Things to improve

| BLOG CONTENT | TRAFFIC |
| --- | --- |
| | |
| MARKETING | MONETIZATION |
| | |

# November →

MONTH:                                    YEAR:

# NOVEMBER
## Overview

| MON | TUE | WED | THU | FRI | SAT | SUN |
|-----|-----|-----|-----|-----|-----|-----|
|     |     |     |     |     |     |     |
|     |     |     |     |     |     |     |
|     |     |     |     |     |     |     |
|     |     |     |     |     |     |     |
|     |     |     |     |     |     |     |

Notes: _____
_____
_____
_____
_____

DATES: MONTH: YEAR:

# WEEKLY
*planner*

**TO DO:**

○ _____
○ _____
○ _____
○ _____
○ _____
○ _____
○ _____
○ _____
○ _____
○ _____

**PRIORITIES**

*Notes:* _____
_____
_____
_____
_____

DATES:  MONTH:  YEAR:

# WEEKLY *planner*

**TO DO:**

- ○ _____
- ○ _____
- ○ _____
- ○ _____
- ○ _____
- ○ _____
- ○ _____
- ○ _____
- ○ _____
- ○ _____

**PRIORITIES**

*Notes:* _____
_____
_____
_____

DATES: MONTH: YEAR:

# WEEKLY
*planner*

**TO DO:**
- ○ _____
- ○ _____
- ○ _____
- ○ _____
- ○ _____
- ○ _____
- ○ _____
- ○ _____
- ○ _____
- ○ _____

**PRIORITIES**

*Notes:* _____
_____
_____
_____
_____

DATES: MONTH: YEAR:

# WEEKLY *planner*

**TO DO:**

○ _____
○ _____
○ _____
○ _____
○ _____
○ _____
○ _____
○ _____
○ _____
○ _____

**PRIORITIES**

*Notes:* _____
_____
_____
_____

# November REVENUE

| AFFILIATE SALES | AMOUNT | DATE |
|---|---|---|
|  |  |  |
|  |  |  |
|  |  |  |
|  |  |  |
|  |  |  |
|  |  |  |
|  |  |  |
|  |  |  |
|  |  |  |
|  |  |  |

**TOTAL AFFILIATE INCOME**

| AD REVENUE | AMOUNT | DATE |
|---|---|---|
|  |  |  |
|  |  |  |
|  |  |  |
|  |  |  |

**TOTAL AD INCOME**

| SERVICES & OFFERS | AMOUNT | DATE |
|---|---|---|
|  |  |  |
|  |  |  |
|  |  |  |
|  |  |  |
|  |  |  |
|  |  |  |
|  |  |  |
|  |  |  |
|  |  |  |
|  |  |  |

**SERVICES INCOME**

| PRODUCT SALES | AMOUNT | DATE |
|---|---|---|
|  |  |  |
|  |  |  |
|  |  |  |
|  |  |  |
|  |  |  |
|  |  |  |
|  |  |  |

**TOTAL SALES**

| SPONSORED WORK | AMOUNT | DATE |
|---|---|---|
|  |  |  |
|  |  |  |
|  |  |  |
|  |  |  |
|  |  |  |
|  |  |  |
|  |  |  |
|  |  |  |
|  |  |  |
|  |  |  |

**SPONSORED INCOME**

| OTHER INCOME | AMOUNT | DATE |
|---|---|---|
|  |  |  |
|  |  |  |
|  |  |  |

**ADDITIONAL INCOME**

**TOTAL NOVEMBER INCOME**

# *November* EXPENSES

| EXPENSE | AMOUNT | DATE |
|---------|--------|------|
|         |        |      |
|         |        |      |
|         |        |      |
|         |        |      |
|         |        |      |
|         |        |      |
|         |        |      |
|         |        |      |
|         |        |      |
|         |        |      |
|         |        |      |
|         |        |      |
|         |        |      |
|         |        |      |
|         |        |      |
|         |        |      |
|         |        |      |
|         |        |      |
|         |        |      |
|         |        |      |

**TOTAL EXPENSES**

# Your **NOVEMBER** review

**PROFIT**

**BIGGEST WIN**

**GOAL**

**ARTICLES**

## BLOG TRAFFIC

| | |
|---|---|
| SESSIONS | |
| PAGE VIEWS | |
| USERS | |
| ORGANIC SESSIONS | |
| PINTEREST SESSIONS | |
| AVR TIME DURATION | |

## SOCIAL GROWTH

| | STARTING NUMBERS | AT THE END of the month | GROWTH |
|---|---|---|---|
| ✉ | | | |
| P | | | |
| 🐦 | | | |
| f | | | |
| 📷 | | | |
| ▶ | | | |
| | | | |

**TAKEAWAYS**

# MONTHLY
*musings*

What worked for my blogging business this month

○ _____
○ _____
○ _____
○ _____
○ _____

*Things to improve*

| BLOG CONTENT | TRAFFIC |
| --- | --- |
| MARKETING | MONETIZATION |

*December* →

MONTH: YEAR:

# DECEMBER
## *Overview*

| MON | TUE | WED | THU | FRI | SAT | SUN |
|-----|-----|-----|-----|-----|-----|-----|
|     |     |     |     |     |     |     |
|     |     |     |     |     |     |     |
|     |     |     |     |     |     |     |
|     |     |     |     |     |     |     |
|     |     |     |     |     |     |     |

Notes: _____
_____
_____
_____

DATES:　　　　　　MONTH:　　　　　　YEAR:

# WEEKLY *planner*

## TO DO:

○ _____
○ _____
○ _____
○ _____
○ _____
○ _____
○ _____
○ _____
○ _____
○ _____

## PRIORITIES

*Notes:* _____
_____
_____
_____
_____

DATES: MONTH: YEAR:

# WEEKLY
*planner*

**TO DO:**

○ _____
○ _____
○ _____
○ _____
○ _____
○ _____
○ _____
○ _____
○ _____
○ _____

**PRIORITIES**

*Notes:* _____
_____
_____
_____

DATES: MONTH: YEAR:

# WEEKLY *planner*

**TO DO:**
- ○ _____
- ○ _____
- ○ _____
- ○ _____
- ○ _____
- ○ _____
- ○ _____
- ○ _____
- ○ _____
- ○ _____

**PRIORITIES**

*Notes:* _____

DATES: MONTH: YEAR:

# WEEKLY
*planner*

**TO DO:**

○ _____
○ _____
○ _____
○ _____
○ _____
○ _____
○ _____
○ _____
○ _____
○ _____

**PRIORITIES**

*Notes:* _____
_____
_____
_____
_____

# *December* REVENUE

| AFFILIATE SALES | AMOUNT | DATE |
|---|---|---|
| | | |
| | | |
| | | |
| | | |
| | | |
| | | |
| | | |
| | | |
| | | |
| | | |
| | | |

**TOTAL AFFILIATE INCOME**

| AD REVENUE | AMOUNT | DATE |
|---|---|---|
| | | |
| | | |
| | | |

**TOTAL AD INCOME**

| SERVICES & OFFERS | AMOUNT | DATE |
|---|---|---|
|  |  |  |
|  |  |  |
|  |  |  |
|  |  |  |
|  |  |  |
|  |  |  |
|  |  |  |
|  |  |  |
|  |  |  |

**SERVICES INCOME**

| PRODUCT SALES | AMOUNT | DATE |
|---|---|---|
|  |  |  |
|  |  |  |
|  |  |  |
|  |  |  |
|  |  |  |
|  |  |  |
|  |  |  |

**TOTAL SALES**

| SPONSORED WORK | AMOUNT | DATE |
|---|---|---|
| | | |
| | | |
| | | |
| | | |
| | | |
| | | |
| | | |
| | | |
| | | |
| | | |

**SPONSORED INCOME**

| OTHER INCOME | AMOUNT | DATE |
|---|---|---|
| | | |
| | | |
| | | |

**ADDITIONAL INCOME**

**TOTAL DECEMBER INCOME**

# December
# EXPENSES

| EXPENSE | AMOUNT | DATE |
|---------|--------|------|
|         |        |      |
|         |        |      |
|         |        |      |
|         |        |      |
|         |        |      |
|         |        |      |
|         |        |      |
|         |        |      |
|         |        |      |
|         |        |      |
|         |        |      |
|         |        |      |
|         |        |      |
|         |        |      |
|         |        |      |
|         |        |      |
|         |        |      |
|         |        |      |
|         |        |      |

**TOTAL EXPENSES**

# Your DECEMBER review

## PROFIT

## BIGGEST WIN

## GOAL

## ARTICLES

## BLOG TRAFFIC

| | |
|---|---|
| SESSIONS | |
| PAGE VIEWS | |
| USERS | |
| ORGANIC SESSIONS | |
| PINTEREST SESSIONS | |
| AVR TIME DURATION | |
| | |

## SOCIAL GROWTH

| | STARTING NUMBERS | AT THE END of the month | GROWTH |
|---|---|---|---|
| ✉ | | | |
| P | | | |
| T | | | |
| F | | | |
| IG | | | |
| ▶ | | | |
| | | | |

## TAKEAWAYS

# MONTHLY
*musings*

### What worked for my blogging business this month

- _____
- _____
- _____
- _____
- _____

## Things to improve

| BLOG CONTENT | TRAFFIC |
|---|---|
|  |  |
| **MARKETING** | **MONETIZATION** |
|  |  |

*Review your year* →

# Your year in REVIEW

**GOALS YOU MET THIS YEAR**

**GOALS YOU DIDN'T MET (YET)**

**LESSONS LEARNED THIS YEAR**

**GOALS FOR NEXT YEAR**

Notes: _____
_____
_____
_____
_____

# MY SUCCESSES
*this year*

# Notes

# ABOUT THE AUTHOR

Ana Skyes is a blogging growth strategist and coach over at www.TheSheApproach.com where she helps content creators increase their blog traffic and revenue using smart blogging strategies.

She is a believer that you shouldn't take your blog numbers personally, but that you definitely should learn from them.

And tracking these key statistics that she included in this planner helped her and her blog coaching clients build several successful blogging and online businesses. So you can yoo!

## Connect with Ana

Main blog: www.TheSheApproach.com

Courses & eBooks: www.TheSheApproach.com/shop

Amazon book: www.TheSheApproach.com/book

Write to her: info@thesheapproach.com

Youtube channel: www.youtube.com/c/AnaTheSheApproach

Free Facebook group: www.facebook.com/groups/smartblogging